M000078078

(ASTROLOGY GEMS)

VIRGO
August 23 – September 22

Monte Farber & Amy Zerner

Sterling Publishing Co., Inc.
New York

Text © 2006 by Monte Farber
Art © 2006 by Amy Zerner

10 9 8 7 6 5 4 3 2 1

Published by Sterling Publishing Co., Inc.
387 Park Avenue South, New York, NY 10016

Distributed in Canada by Sterling Publishing
c/o Canadian Manda Group, 165 Dufferin Street
Toronto, Ontario, Canada M6K 3H6

Distributed in the United Kingdom by GMC
Distribution Services
Castle Place, 166 High Street, Lewes, East Sussex,
England BN7 1XU

Distributed in Australia by Capricorn Link (Australia)
Pty. Ltd.
P.O. Box 704, Windsor, NSW 2756, Australia

Printed in China

Sterling ISBN-13: 978-1-4027-4186-9
         ISBN-10: 1-4027-4186-3

For information about custom editions, special sales,
premium and corporate purchases, please contact
Sterling Special Sales Department at 800-805-5489 or
specialsales@sterlingpub.com.

What's Your Sign?

When someone asks you "What's your sign?" you know what that person really means is "What's your astrological sign?" Professional astrologers more often use the phrase "Sun sign," a term reflecting the concept that a person's sign is determined by which of the twelve signs of the zodiac the Sun appeared to be passing through at the moment she was born. The zodiac is the narrow band of sky circling the Earth's equator through which the Sun, the Moon, and the planets appear to move when viewed by us here on Earth.

Astrology's Gift

Astrology, which has been around for thousands of years, is the study of how planetary positions relate to earthly events and people. Its long and rich history has resulted in a wealth of philosophical and psychological wisdom, the basic concepts of which we are going to share with you in the pages of this book. As the Greek philosopher Heracleitus (c. 540–c. 480 BCE) said, "Character is destiny." Who you are—complete with all of your goals, tendencies, habits, virtues, and vices—will

determine how you act and react, thereby creating your life's destiny. Like astrology itself, our Astrology Gems series is designed to help you to better know yourself and those you care about. You will then be better able to use your free will to shape your life to your liking.

Does Astrology Work?

Many people rightly question how astrology can divide humanity into twelve Sun signs and make predictions that can be correct for everyone of the same sign. The simple answer is that it cannot do that—that's newspaper astrology, entertaining but not the real thing. Rather, astrology can help you understand your strengths and weaknesses so that you can better accept yourself as you are and use your strengths to compensate for your weaknesses. Real astrology is designed to help you to become yourself fully.

Remember, virtually all the music in the history of Western music has been composed using variations of the same twelve notes. Similarly, the twelve Sun signs of astrology are basic themes rich with meaning that each of us expresses differently to create and respond to the unique opportunities and challenges of our life.

August 23–September 22

Planet
Mercury

Element
Earth

Quality
Mutable

Day
Wednesday

Season
summer

Colors
navy blue, gray, green, tan

Plants
fern, chrysanthemum, sage

Perfume
patchouli

Gemstones
apatite, aventurine, white opal,
peridot

Metal
mercury

Personal qualities
Conservative, discreet, practical,
intelligent, and detail oriented

We call the following words "keywords" because they can help you unlock the core meaning of the astrological sign of Virgo. Each keyword represents issues and ideas that are of supreme importance and prominence in the lives of people born with Virgo as their Sun sign. You will usually find that every Virgo embodies at least one of these keywords in the way she makes a living:

thought · observation · study

analysis · discrimination

division into component parts

criticism · reason · logic

connection · adaptation

moving things about · spreading

making by hand · crafting

forming · detail · prediction

calculation · symbolism

translation · communication

speech · writing and reading

Virgo's Symbolic Meaning

Virgo is usually depicted as a young woman holding shafts of wheat. While Virgo is commonly thought of as "the virgin," it is important to note that in ancient times the word "virgin" actually had two meanings: it was used not only to refer to a sexually inexperienced individual, but also to describe an independent woman who did things on her own terms and over whom no man held dominion. Indeed, Virgos thrive when they are able to do things in their own way.

The dual meaning of the word "virgin" reflects the dual nature that most Virgos exhibit. Sometimes they are completely confident in their opinions and competence, but at other times they are as filled with self-doubt and naïveté as a young beginner. This aspect of their character correlates perfectly with the fact that Virgo is one of the four Mutable, or changeable, signs of astrology (the other three being Gemini, Pisces, and Sagittarius).

The Sun passes through the Mutable signs of the zodiac when we here on Earth are preparing for the change of seasons, and people born during the time of these Mutable signs are therefore considered to be highly adaptable under a variety of circumstances. Flexible and open to change, such individuals deal with each situation depending on the needs and desires of the moment. Virgos are more comfortable adapting to outside influences than they are imposing their will on others.

The shafts of wheat held by the strong young woman represent Virgo's connection with the Earth; this is key because Virgo is an Earth sign—one of three Sun signs focused on physical well-being and the practical matters of daily life (the other two Earth signs are Taurus and Capricorn). The element of Earth symbolizes logic, dependability, and a sense of duty to those who are considered valuable and worthy. People born during the time that the Sun is traveling through one of the three Earth signs are the most reliable and responsible. They have their feet on the ground and possess a practical gift for understanding the material world.

The wheat that Virgo holds is also symbolic of the harvest—the time of year during which a Virgo's birthday falls. In agrarian societies, harvesttime was the busiest and most important time of the year—hence, Virgo's hardworking tendencies.

Recognizing a Virgo

People who exhibit the physical characteristics distinctive of the sign of Virgo look neat and fastidious and have a pleasant, often quietly beautiful face. They are not usually noisy people or the kind to call attention to themselves on purpose, though their version of what looks right and proper is often unique, so that it appears as though they're dressing to confront other people's values—but they're not!

Virgo's Typical Behavior and Personality Traits

- capable of analyzing situations in detail
- basically shy, no matter how talkative
- unsentimental and unemotional
- serves others in some way
- defines herself through work
- feels a little insecure
- notices and remembers details

- efficient and orderly
- helpful with practical matters
- does not express feelings easily
- can be critical or perfectionistic
- takes responsibilities seriously

What Makes a Virgo Tick?

Virgos are driven by the search for perfection in every way. This quest is apparent in everything they do or say—and especially in what they don't (or won't) do or say. In fact, they would rather do nothing than do the wrong thing, which often leads others to misinterpret their behavior as procrastination. But at the heart of the typical Virgo is the hardest worker you've ever met—ready, willing, and able to help anyone he deems worthy of his service.

The Virgo Personality Expressed Positively

Virgos who are driven to perform useful acts to the best of their abilities display the skillful, hardworking, and humble personality of their sign. Their ability to successfully solve any problem by paying close attention to the smallest of details is due to their ability to analyze people, situations, and procedures. They can analyze anything and devise a way to make it better.

On a Positive Note

Virgos displaying the positive characteristics associated with their sign also tend to be:

- ✸ gentle
- ✸ organized
- ✸ sympathetic
- ✸ humane
- ✸ high energy
- ✸ witty and charming
- ✸ knowledgeable about good health
- ✸ helpful
- ✸ dedicated

The Virgo Personality Expressed Negatively

Virgos who are unable to stop themselves from worrying about everyone and everything display the self-limiting tendency of their sign. They can get so bogged down attending to unimportant details that they miss the big picture. While they may express criticism with the best of intentions, this action can get them into trouble (and when their criticism is expressed with less-than-noble intentions, the ensuing trouble is that much greater).

Negative Traits

Virgos displaying the negative characteristics associated with their sign also tend to be:

- cranky and irritable
- dogmatic and harshly critical
- untidy
- hypochondriacal
- nervous and worried
- prudish
- overly demanding
- undemonstrative

Ask a Virgo If…

Ask a Virgo if you want to know the latest news and gossip, or if you want to know where to find the best of the best, from restaurants to theater. The importance that Virgos place on perfection leads them to seek out the crème de la crème in all sorts of areas in life. Their taste in all things is legendary, and if they are not artists or craftspeople themselves, they make good, though sometimes harsh, critics.

Virgos As Friends

Some of the best qualities possessed by Virgos are kindness, honesty, and a strong sense of responsibility. So it's not surprising that they tend to make great friends. And they can be extremely helpful friends to have, as Virgos need the opportunity to be useful to others and are at their best if they are allowed to take charge of as many apparently mundane matters as you can throw at them.

When it comes to making friends, Virgos are usually drawn to people who are tidy, clean, and intelligent. What's more, they tend to appreciate those who have a broad range of interests. Virgos tend to stay away from individuals given to big shows of emotion, preferring instead to spend time with those who offer a sense of peace and serenity.

Looking for Love

Virgos' quest for perfection extends to their love lives as well. The typical Virgo not only wants her partner to be perfect, but sets this benchmark for the way in which they get together, too. This can lead to wonderful, romantic interludes with fascinating people, but it can also lead to endless lonely nights if Virgos allow their impossibly high standards to prevent them from getting to know someone. Indeed, Virgos tend to be extremely picky about whom they get close to physically and emotionally. It is common to find a Virgo spending long periods without a love interest, but then suddenly moving in with someone who has passed all the tests she can throw at him.

Setting a high mark for others, however, is not the biggest obstacle Virgos face in finding a soul mate, nor is a fear of intimacy. Rather, the biggest stumbling block on Virgo's path to true love is the fear that once she has let a love interest get close, that person will discover that she is not perfect and will ultimately leave.

The way for a Virgo to keep a romantic relationship on track is not only to be aware of this tendency in herself, but also to share it with a potential partner if it starts to become a problem. The good news is that this particular worry of Virgo's is often found to be quite endearing by those who fall in love with them.

Finding That Special Someone

As Virgos tend to be discriminating, displaying a fine artistic taste and a wealth of knowledge on many subjects, museums, lectures, classes, food or wine tastings, galleries, concerts, and even libraries are the kinds of venues where Virgos can be at their best and ready to meet others.

First Dates

Virgos love pageantry. What's more, they delight in companions who share this love of fanfare. An ideal night out might involve tickets to the opera, with dinner at a restaurant known for its decor as well as its menu. Virgos like tasting-size portions and are usually delighted to order a number of small dishes so that a variety of intriguing delicacies may be sampled. After the evening is over, a Virgo remembers every costume and set change in the opera and is happy to recount them—as well as what she and her date wore, said, and did (and why)—in detail to friends.

Virgo in Love

Virgo is the most practical romantic in the zodiac. He is shy and slow to love because self-doubt and low self-esteem make him resistant to believing that someone could love him—even when that person genuinely thinks he's the best thing she's ever encountered. Though logical and analytical, a Virgo is not interested in anything less than the kind of true love found in fairy tales. When he falls in love, he will love intensely.

Undying Love

Forget one-night stands—they are all too often highly forgettable. Virgos are better off looking for a life of quality and meaning spent with a person to whom they are proud to be both a soul mate and a helpmate. Once they find love, their feelings will grow warmly and steadily, along with their devotion to their partner. What's more, having finally decided that a person is worthy of their affections, Virgos, characteristically shy and gentle, can demonstrate an almost volcanic passion that can become a central force in their formerly all-work-and-no-play lives.

Expectations in Love

Virgos expect the same 100 percent level of devotion from a committed partner that they themselves are always striving to give. But not everyone is capable of demonstrating such devotion, so Virgos can become disappointed in their partners for not reciprocating at an equal level and, as a result, can start to question the imbalance in the relationship. However, once Virgos accept that this is simply the way things are—that they are able to give much more than others can—they can return to giving 100 percent without reservation.

Virgos have a highly developed sense of decency and loyalty that they expect their partners to respect and emulate. Most are so committed to doing right by their partners that they are highly resistant to the charms of others and will never stray.

Virgos expect to be fussed over by their partners when they are feeling down. They also expect their personal matters, especially their faults and failings, to be kept private. Last but not least, they expect their feelings to be handled with tender loving care.

What Virgos Look For

Virgos are not looking for someone to cater to their every whim, nor are they likely to be dazzled by sexy makeup and clothes. Obvious good looks are not what attracts them to a potential partner; rather, it's what lies beneath the surface that matters to them. They appreciate a stellar person whose invaluable, wonderful qualities may be known only by them. This can sometimes lead friends and family to be confounded by their choice of partners.

If Virgos Only Knew…

If Virgos only knew the high regard others hold them in, they would realize that, as imperfect as they consider themselves to be, they're a lot closer to perfection than the rest of us! Those lucky enough to have a Virgo love interest are usually those seeking the best that life has to offer, which is why it is not unusual for two Virgos to get together; such a union is a unique experience for the rest of the world to observe, but it's not that unusual an occurrence.

Marriage

True to their analytical nature, Virgos approach a marriage proposal with great caution, weighing the pros and cons thoroughly before popping the question or giving an answer. While this behavior may sound cold and clinical, Virgos approach important life decisions in a methodical, thoughtful manner.

Those involved with a Virgo cannot expect a miraculous transformation after engagement or marriage. If anything, once Virgos are comfortable and secure in a relationship, they make an even greater effort to be perfect—as a tribute to their love.

A Virgo marriage ceremony will be either an affair worthy of magazine coverage or an elopement—nothing in between. Either every last detail will be made as perfect as possible or the pageantry will be dispensed with entirely, thereby saving the sanity of both parties.

Virgo's Opposite Sign

Pisces is the opposite sign of Virgo. A relationship between Virgo and Pisces can be difficult, but there are certain things that Virgo can learn from Pisces. Pisces can teach Virgo to accept help from another individual instead of giving all the time. Pisces can also show Virgo how to relax that inner critical voice a little and flow with the tide, giving her imagination a chance to develop. In this way, Virgo can begin to accept human imperfections, especially her own.

Pairing Up

In general, if people display the characteristics typical of their sign, intimate relationships between a Virgo and another individual can be described as follows:

Virgo with Virgo
Harmonious; the quest for perfection shared!

Virgo with Libra
Harmonious; such different types, but the relationship works

Virgo with Scorpio
Harmonious, as long as the Scorpio is boss

Virgo with Sagittarius
Difficult because respect is lacking

Virgo with Capricorn
Harmonious, with both partners
contributing to make it work

Virgo with Aquarius
Difficult, filled with arguments that
neither lover hears

Virgo with Pisces
Harmonious because opposites attract,
but then what?

Virgo with Aries
Turbulent as lovers, but good
as friends

Virgo with Taurus
Harmonious and secure—first class!

Virgo with Gemini
Difficult; Virgo practicality versus Gemini theories and fancies

Virgo with Cancer
Harmonious; a true partnership of caring individuals

Virgo with Leo
Harmonious; oh so different, yet the relationship can work!

If Things Don't Work Out

Virgos are typically loyal and will avoid ending a marriage or other permanent relationship whenever possible. However, in the long run, Virgos are sensible, practical people. If Virgo's sense of fair play has been outraged, he will make a quick and final break. Since a Virgo usually has good self-discipline, the past is soon put aside in favor of moving on to a new chapter.

Virgo at Work

A whole book could be written just about Virgos and work because they love it and are so good at it. Even the most career-oriented Virgo takes it one job at a time, a trait that gets her noticed by superiors as the go-to person in every situation. Unfortunately, this characteristic sometimes makes it hard for Virgos to advance to better jobs because they are seen as being essential to the job they already have. Their tendency to be humble often adds to this drag on their career and must be addressed, especially if the goal is to climb the corporate ladder.

Virgos' shrewd use of logic and incisive understanding, coupled with their ability to communicate their insights well, make them essential to the success of enterprises large and small. They are the soul of efficiency and can analyze any system, laying bare its strengths and weaknesses and allowing a better system to be created. Their strength of character will not let them leave a project before it is finished, so if you ask them for help, let them help and don't expect them to stop until they think the job is finished.

To most Virgos, career plans and the expansion of existing projects are not as interesting as the details of everything they are already committed to. Virgos believe that every little job that they're involved with is equally important to their overall career. Although others might be able to get away with ignoring such matters, it is important for Virgos to pay special attention to pleasantries and minor rules and regulations. It is also important that they pay close attention to the precise meanings of words used in speech and writing, as well as the interpretation of policies.

Typical Occupations

A Virgo is well suited for any occupation that enables him to give service and handle complicated or difficult details. Health care, chemistry, pharmacology, engineering, accounting, programming, and architecture come to mind immediately, but there are many other careers where Virgo's precise manner and keen eye can come in handy. Quality control is a field where the sign's skill set can be put to especially good use. And arts that require masterful eye-hand coordination will provide much pleasure.

Really, Virgos can excel at virtually any pursuit they put their mind to, as long as it involves creative analysis rather than long-term business goals. The best type of job for Virgos involves breaking things down into their component parts and analyzing them.

Details, Details

Virgo is detail oriented and will make lists of things to do, executing them one by one. She remembers dates and agreements to the letter. She can be a wizard when it comes to the sensible balancing of the budget. She loves her work, honors her commitments, and criticizes everything—to make it better, of course.

Virgo is shy but as tough as nails when the need arises. In business, she is cool, intelligent, and fully committed. Virgos often meet their romantic partners through their job or profession. They feel more like themselves when they are fully engaged in their work than at practically any other time.

Of all the signs, Virgos are the most adept at suppressing their feelings and emotions for fear that they may be seen as weak. They are thus quick to criticize decisions based purely on "gut instinct," preferring logical analysis instead. For this reason, a Virgo is best off working with individuals who are able to counter the Virgo's point of view with gentle but forceful insistence that intuition is the complement to logic, not its antithesis.

Behavior and Abilities at Work

In the workplace, a typical Virgo:

- keeps everyone focused on details

- helps people in trouble or who ask for assistance

- displays meticulousness and self-discipline

- gives others a sense of stability

- enjoys complicated, routine tasks

Virgo As Employer

A typical Virgo boss:

- practices full disclosure
- demonstrates good manners
- remembers everything
- expects fairness from others
- expects good grooming and good habits
- handles complicated projects with aplomb
- rewards good work with pay, not perks
- leads by consensus

Virgo As Employee

A typical Virgo employee:

- ✤ has an inquiring, logical mind

- ✤ possesses excellent research and writing skills

- ✤ expects to be paid well

- ✤ demonstrates courtesy, reliability, and thoroughness

- ✤ works in a cautious, critical, and methodical fashion

Virgo As Coworker

Virgos take their professional relationships seriously, combining duty with
devotion. Loyal and committed, they
tend to develop the kind of bonds with
coworkers that are more often found
among family members.

Money

Virgos have the ability to attain any reward they work for diligently and patiently. Being practical ensures that Virgos have enough when they need it the most. Fortunately, Virgos do not succumb to the temptation of immediate gratification. And while they tend to wait until they can afford the best, they won't break themselves to do so. Virgos save their resources for the future. These resources are not always money or wealth in the material sense, though they often are. What Virgos consider necessary for their own success is what is important. These necessities can take the form of family connections, friendships, favors owed, and even secrets shared. The strength of their faith, in terms of religion and what they are committed to, is as important as any material resource.

At Home

Virgos thrive at home, as they are the most relaxed in their own space. They prefer to putter around, fixing, tidying, and tending to household chores, rather than being out and about. They are usually either compulsively neat or total slobs. Virgos often have prized collections of things, sometimes things others might consider odd things to collect.

Behavior and Abilities at Home

Virgo typically:

✺ enjoys planning and fixing

✺ is adept in such areas as cooking, management of general maintenance, and gardening

✺ likes to be doing or making something instead of sitting around idly

✺ pursues several hobbies at or from home

Leisure Interests

Most Virgos enjoy engaging in intellectual pursuits and hands-on hobbies during their free time. Restless by nature, they need plenty of activities to keep them occupied. They are not, however, naturally inclined toward sports, though many exercise regularly for the sake of their health.

The typical Virgo enjoys the following pastimes:

❋ playing with the latest high-tech gadgets

❋ attending concerts and plays

❋ gardening

❋ reading books and magazines

❋ creating detailed craft projects

❋ engaging in needlework or model making

❋ taking self-improvement courses

Virgoan Likes

- lists and plans and punctuality
- nice soaps
- small animals
- flowers and herbs
- name brands of high quality
- healthy foods
- beautiful serving plates
- interesting collections
- ingenious storage bins and boxes
- muted colors

Virgoan Dislikes

* crowds, noise, and brash people
* slang and cursing
* dirt and disorder
* people who complain a lot
* sitting still for a long time
* disrupted routines
* lids left off boxes, or tops off toothpaste
* being obligated to others
* having their personal things moved by others
* bright, bold, primary colors

The Secret Side of Virgo

Inside anyone who has strong Virgo influences is a tendency to worry too much about every personal imperfection and to never be satisfied with her own standards. A Virgo may appear on the surface to be a know-it-all and a compulsive worker, but these aspects of her personality mask a deep fear that she is not good enough, especially for her job or her partner.

Mercury ☿

Mercury, the planet of the mind and communication, rules the sign of Virgo, so those born under this sign are mentally quick, incisive, and sharp. Drawn to education—both teaching and learning—Virgos are particularly interested in computers.

Thanks to Mercury's strong association with communication (in Roman mythology, the god Mercury was known as the "winged messenger"), Virgos are good at keeping in touch. Great correspondents, they enjoy sending letters and e-mail. What's more, they're witty and wonderful conversationalists, able to recount and act out whole scenarios and events in detail.

Bringing Up a Young Virgo

Young Virgos need plenty of hugs and sincere compliments every day to build self-confidence—a trait that Virgos typically are not born with. Young Virgos try very hard to please, as long as they know clearly what is expected of them.

As they grow up, Virgos often find close relationships with the opposite sex challenging. Offering them much genuine praise and encouragement early in life will help to smooth the path to true love in the teenage years and early adulthood. It takes a lot of convincing to make Virgos believe they are physically attractive people and worthy of love, as they are extremely self-critical.

On the whole, young Virgos strive for good grades at school and help out around the house. Exacting about time, food, and orderliness, they tend to be extremely neat, almost to a fault, when it comes to their belongings. An untidy Virgo will have some other strong influence countering her Sun sign in her astrological birth chart.

Virgo children have a tendency to be critical about everyone else in the family, especially when asked for an opinion. They therefore need to be taught to accept other people's foibles and not to get upset about little things that aren't important.

Virgo As a Parent

The typical Virgo parent:

- encourages children to ask questions

- supports practical activities during free time

- worries about the children's health

- may find it hard to express affection warmly

- gets upset by children's dirt and untidiness

- explains the demands he makes

- does anything to help his children

The Virgo Child

The typical Virgo child:

- is quick and alert

- is an excellent mimic

- can learn many things in a short time

- is often an early talker and reader

- gets upset if she forgets something that she previously memorized

- rarely questions authority

- frequently questions facts

- is honest and reliable

- ✳ demonstrates shyness with strangers
- ✳ loves to do jobs around the home, imitating an adult
- ✳ can be a fussy eater
- ✳ tends to be tidy, with occasional bouts of disorganization
- ✳ gets very upset if teased

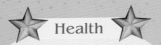

Health

Virgos are typically healthy and usually take good care of themselves. However, if terribly worried or unhappy, they may succumb to their sign's tendency toward hypochondria.

Virgos can experience frequent stom-achaches stemming from their anxious, nervous nature. To maintain their health, they should be wary of working too much and instead learn to

relax. However, Virgos
often have to trick them-
selves into relaxing by thinking of it
as one more job on their long to-do
list. They should sleep more, and spend
as much time as possible walking out-
doors. Virgos should also avoid alcohol and
foods that are very spicy.

⭐ FAMOUS VIRGOS ⭐

Fiona Apple

Lauren Bacall

Leonard Bernstein

Andrea Bocelli

Sean Connery

Cameron Diaz

Greta Garbo

Richard Gere

Faith Hill

Michael Jackson

Jesse James

Lyndon B. Johnson

B.B. King

Stephen King

Sophia Loren

Marlee Matlin

Bill Murray

Bob Newhart

Otis Redding

Keanu Reeves

Jada Pinkett Smith

Mother Teresa

Lily Tomlin

Twiggy

Luke Wilson

About the Authors

Internationally known self-help author Monte Farber's inspiring guidance and empathic insights impact everyone he encounters. Amy Zerner's exquisite one-of-a-kind spiritual couture creations and collaged fabric paintings exude her profound intuition and deep connection with archetypal stories and healing energies. Together, they have built The Enchanted World of Amy Zerner and Monte Farber: books, card decks, and

oracles that have helped millions discover their own spiritual paths.

Their best-selling titles include The Chakra Meditation Kit, The Enchanted Tarot, The Instant Tarot Reader, The Psychic Circle, Karma Cards, The Truth Fairy, The Healing Deck, True Love Tarot, Animal Powers Meditation Kit, The Breathe Easy Deck, The Pathfinder Psychic Talking Board, and Gifts of the Goddess Affirmation Cards.

For further information, please visit: **www.TheEnchantedWorld.com**